GOOD

GOOD AND EVIL

In all I see, I see death
Evil
In all I think, I become confused
Disillusioned
Ignorant to the true truth
Good and Evil

In all I seek I do find, but yet that more I truly cannot find.

Yes there is a void
That empty space between real and unreal.
There is a great divide that can be explained but yet, it cannot due to complication.

So as I think of life, I truly have to think of good and evil and that great big choice.

Michelle

GOOD AND EVIL

You know Lovey its funny how evil still lingers around me. It's amazing how I cannot shake the evil forces that surrounds me; infiltrates my dream world and home.

I truly do not know what to do now because you're truly not hearing me. I need my good and true freedom from the evils' that plague my life and world.

Lovey I truly don't know anymore because along the way I've missed the big picture with you.

You were trying to show me something; I get it, but I truly did not get it.

Both good and evil are from the same foundation, but yet in all of my asking I realize that good and evil want and need the same thing.

Good definitely do not want to be around evil and evil do not want to be around good. They both hate each other and this I am finding out now.

Lovey why did I not figure this out all along?

After all the books that I've written; why now?

Why let me find this out now?

Good and Evil want their separate space; so why not give it to them?

Why keep both sides living in vain Lovey?

Why keep both sides living together or in close proximity to each other?

Lovey, Good and Evil truly do not get along and neither side can find a common ground to live with each other; so why keep good and evil together?

Separate the two. This is best; this separation is best for both sides. Under no circumstances must you keep them together anymore. There is strife and the death toll and hatred is truly not worth it Lovey come on now.

Someone hate and despise me, why would I want to be around them or even live close to them? Come on now.

Good want all evil to disappear and Evil want all good to disappear; die?

So why not create a solid foundation with both Lovey? I mean, why not give good their world where no evil can come in?

Why not give evil their world where not good can come in? This can be done Lovey because it is done in the spiritual realm; so why not here on earth?

Keep both worlds separate and apart so that neither side can get to the other no matter how hard they try.

Now I have to ask you this Lovey, why did you ask me to write a book when it's death for death? Meaning evil wants good dead and in truth; good wants evil dead. So both want death for each other why?

No that's a stupid question on my part because I know why. It's like, why does death have to be in the midst of it all?

What is the purpose of good over evil when good is preeing death for evil and vise versa?

So Lovey, who am I?

Am I any better than evil Lovey?
Am I?

Am I not like evil because I want all facets of sin and evil gone forever ever without end more than infinitely an indefinitely from the earth, universe and spiritual realm and wherever good life resides?

So now tell me, how am I fair and just in all of this?

I have to question my logic and sense Lovey.

Good over evil I say, but isn't evil saying the same thing; evil over good?

So what right do I have to condemn and say Lovey? What right do I have?

Am I not as guilty as everyone else?
Am I not as wrong and unjust as them?

Many questions I have Lovey and only you can answer them for me. Yes the state of mind is different but you know what Lovey; I leave all to you because **_"ALL THINGS ARE WORKING."_** Fred Hammond

I truly won't let evil take me from you because you are my good and true right Lovey. So truly hold on to me and not hand me over to death. I trust you because you are my hope, dreams and good desire and I will not let you go. You are good to me thus you are around me just like my mother. So truly secure my mother and all you've given me in goodness and in truth for always.

Michelle

Ah Lovey can we truly take Russia off our agenda because of her?

Too much Babylonian history rooted there. So can we good and truly take this land off our to go to list of goodness and truth. Yes Lovey this is my good and true will on your day, December 29, 2015. I truly need goodness for me and you and this land I truly want to forfeit. Yes there was something pulling me there and after seeing what I saw; I truly don't want to go there. It makes no sense now; nor would it be in our best interest in my good and true book.

I truly cannot go there knowing the deep Babylonian roots there for real.

It's sad that a country that claims purity and or wanting to keep their lineage pure truly do not know their true lineage and true history. Thus the history and lineage of man is distorted and corrupt. Babylon has and have influenced the world; glove, thus their lies and deceit have not stopped.

We are being brainwashed into believing they are pure and holy thus forgetting that the forbidding that you did when it came to them; mixing seed (genes), culture, clothing, language, thinking, praise, truth, land and so much more with them. Now history; the history of man has been distorted and they are included in the lying history books of man globally. The pitting and hatred has always been there Lovey; thus good and evil cannot coexist in peace and you truly know this.

Yes this does not concern me. Therefore, I truly thank you for making me the way I am and seeing the real truth of them; this land. Neither black or white know the truth but yet say they do.

Like I've said in other books; I will not hand over your goodness and truth to wicked and evil people. I am not saying these people (Russians) are wicked and evil but due to deep roots; the root and roots of Babylon, I truly cannot in good and true will travel there. So truly take Russia off our to go list for sure.

Lovey, I know if I am wrong in saying this you will correct me, but Lovey the vomit of her marrying him a Babylonian. Disgusting for real; thus let me truly stay in my lane with you and stay on the right path of truth and true love with you and only you. You know what Lovey, man; humans truly do not know what they have done and no matter how you try; they are truly not listening.

Truth must prevail Lovey; thus good over all that is evil always.

Michelle

Lovey, what is going on?

Why is death wreaking havoc in and on my life?

Why can't death leave me alone?

From the 26th onwards death has been in my life and can't leave. Now on your day; the day I gave onto you; death has unleashed it's fury upon me brutal all night long.

<u>Lovey, what part of no part of death do I want and need that you do not comprehend or over stand?</u>

What part of locking death out of my life like you've locked evil from going into the realms of the good and true in the spiritual realm that you do not comprehend or over stand?

Now look, death has handed me my death?

I dreamt I was carrying my death in my hand; death gave me my death and I was carrying it in my hand.

What does this mean Lovey?

<u>Does this mean I am free from death now, or does it mean I am going to die?</u>

Is someone going to die in my family Lovey?

No, someone is going to die; I know this for a fact. Thus my dream world was plagued with nothing but death and more death.

I dreamt I was in this place, this dark place I would call it and or say. I dreamt Cleopatra who had jet black hair and fair skin. More brown and or yellow skin, but not white people skin in hue. <u>**Thus Cleopatra is truly not white as white people would have you think and believe.**</u>

I cannot tell you what she looked like exactly but I know she had black hair and fair skin; brown skin then. The dream is vague Lovey thus I ask you, <u>**where are you in my spiritual world; dream world?**</u>

<u>**Why are you not there to guard and protect me?**</u>

<u>**Why are you not there to defend me and turn back these curses in my life?**</u>

Now I ask you, why are you allowing death to beat up on me so in this our good and true month of December?

Is this month not our true month?

Is this not a month of truth and good giving?
Is this not the month of hope?

Is this not the month that I need and want death to get the hell out of because this month does not belong to death?

So why are you Lovey letting death make December his and her strong hold?

Why are you allowing death and hell to unleash their fury on me?

This is the 29th day of December Lovey, your good and true day, so why is death coming into my home and destroying me like this?

Now dis dutty stinking dead meat wey name Cleopatra wey drangcrow nuh want have the gaul and nerve, audacity fi cum tell me fi worship har.

Lovey, who dis dutty stinking rev out whoring Delilah and sketel wey did tun bed pan fi di Roman Empire tink shi a talk to?

Who the puck is she to come tell me to worship har?

Lovey, this is your day and I know I am not to get upset but live this down and humble myself, but dis dutty stinking crasses a pass har place. Who si bi fi mi fi bow down to har? Dyam wrenk fi real.

Mi fi worship a dutty pussy.

Aundaneath yu stink wussa dan di sulphur pits of earth and hell an mi fi worship yu.

Gyal guh more dan rinse out yuself because not even jayze can help yu. Kibba yuself an chuck literally.

Pucking bright bout mi fi worship yu. I do not worship people. You're a fucking skirt and whore; why the fuck would I want to worship you?

Who the fuck do you think you are?

I do not worship idols. You're a nobody in my book and you're not a fucking idol either for anyone to worship you.

Idols are not to be worshipped.

Humans are not to be worshipped.

Deities are not to be worshipped. I know this; so why would I bow down to you?

You're not in my league. You're a fucking count out so chuck bitch.

 Keep your fucking Babylonian bullshit. You're ugly so get a fucking clue.

GOOD AND EVIL

Lovey don't tell me to worship im anna yu mi fi worship. Egyptian drangcrow goh fine Anubis and chuck and or go fuck yuself? Dyam bright; stink; wrenk. Crowbaite goh learn fi wash yuself because obviously you're not smelling the stench of you; how yu pucking smell fi real.

Death nuh diday with yu? Wey yu noh goh play with him saxophone and blow? Oh I forgot, not even drangcrow want yu; so death truly do not want you because yu stink; worse dan some death literally.

Drangcrow wey drangcrow nuh want; yu noh si sey yu fucking dead and lef a doa. A mi yu waane cum tess. Goh tess yu dutty mumma because har pussy stink jus lacka fi yu if not worse.

Dyam bright. You cannot pass your place with death anna mi yu a cum pass yu place with?

Bitch chuck.

So Lovey, afta di wrenking and stinking gyal wey smell wuss dan ten day ole piss cum tell me dat; mi get mad. I cannot remember if I chucked her and or pushed her, but I told her; "I am not worshipping you." Afta mi tell hard at now, my floral comforter of blue, yellow and white and or creamy white that my last child use to cover at nights was beside me. All I felt was this cut on the lower right side of my back. I could see the cut for some strange reason. No blood came out but in the cut you could see nothing but darkness. Lovey the cut was so strong and powerful that I felt the cut in the living and I woke up out of my sleep.

Lovey what is truly going on in my life?

Did I not dedicate myself to your goodness in goodness and in truth?

Are you telling me now that my life belongs to death?

Is death not handing me back death on your day and I truly do not know why nor do I want it?

If I've given death his and her due; why are they giving me back death?

Why do they continue to interfere with me in my spiritual and physical life and world?

I truly cannot comprehend this Lovey?

I gave you back life Lovey and you gave it back to me. I gave back death is due because I did tell you to let death's people go; give them back to death and now on your day, death is giving me back death. Death is handing me back death Lovey. **SO NOW I ASK YOU LOVEY THIS; DO I HOLD THE KEY TO LIFE AND DEATH?**

AM I THE KEEPER OF LIFE AND DEATH?
Am I the one to die now?
Is it time for me to return to you?

Why did death handing me back death Lovey?

I saw myself carrying death Lovey; why?

Lovey, the comforter means death. I know death is coming in my family, but truly let death pass this family by.

Lovey truly do not let death take any of my children nor let death take my brothers or sister including sisters; the sisters I've never met but heard of.

Lovey truly secure my family for me because they are truly important to me. This cut truly hurt Lovey come on now.

Further, secure my life for me. You know the trouble and troubles that are truly before me and I am asking you to truly secure me in goodness and in truth with you more than infinitely and indefinitely without end in goodness and in truth.

Lovey, why let death unleash death on me so?

Why not secure me?
Why did you not protect me?
Why let death reach me like this?

I also dreamt the legions of doom coming into my home and pretending that they are with me.

Lovey, I care not for the illuminati demons that flood this earth and are in high and powerful places. I do not fear them because life stops at the flesh for them due to the evils that they do. Good and true life cannot end. Good and true life grows up and go up to you Lovey. **_This is why I tell people; never interlock the upright and or upward and downward triangle. Once you interlock the upright and downward triangle you are telling Lovey that you are of the realm of the dead. You gave your life over to death; thus Lovey cannot and will not have anything to do with you. You belong to death and he cannot interfere with the good and true choice you've made._**

The upright eye in the triangle represent spiritual life. The life you go up to once your spirit sheds the flesh if you are good.

It is at this stage and level of life where you are changed to see Lovey in order to dwell with Lovey. Thus many black church goers sing the song, "**_we shall be changed, changed from mortal to immortality in a twinkling of an eye._**" *This song is a true song when it comes to the changing that must take place in order for you to see Life; good and true life, and that life is Lovey. Please note that I saw this*

GOOD AND EVIL

stage as an operation in the spiritual realm; thus I've relayed this information to humanity as I saw it Lovey.

The downward triangle and for some the downward eye in the triangle represent hell; where your spirit go to die after your spirit shed the flesh if you lived a wicked and evil life here on earth. This is where true evil and sinful people go to die. And it matters not if you tried to live your life good and true. **<u>From you have one more sin on your sin record than good; you must go to hell to die. This is why I tell you to know your sins here on earth because the life you live in the living determines where you go in the afterlife; once your spirit sheds the flesh.</u>**

When they (the circles of death) are burning in hell like a bitch with their families; I know I will be safe and secure with you Lovey in your good and true abode. None can call out to me because like I've told you time and time again Lovey, I refuse to save anyone that is wicked and evil. So I truly don't know why death is giving me and or handing me back death. Come on now.

Evil hath nothing to do with me nor does it have anything to do with you Lovey; so truly separate good from evil. We truly cannot coexist nor can we co parent in peace. Evil seek to kill and destroy all that is good so that they can reign supreme with more than an iron fist over anyone that oppose them. Thus here on earth wicked people invade, enslave, destroy and kill. Look at the many nations here on earth that has been colonized and enslaved by wicked and evil people.

Look at the torture and rape; willful murder that the so called white race have done to their own black race in the name of them.

Look at how the Babylonians (Indian Race) took us from you Lovey.

They too enslaved us. Egypt was a testament of this.

They were the first to take us out and or away from you Lovey because of beauty. Thus you showed me the pretty skinned people; Russians. They are the pretty skinned people and in truth Lovey; their skin is pretty to look upon. I am not going to lie to you when it comes to this. Thus I've asked you, if a people that's so cold can be warm?

They (the Babylonians) gave us their false god and gods. Now this bitch wants me to worship her and because I got upset at her and tell her no, she gave me death; cut me so that I felt the cut in the living.

Lovey, you are my good and true choice of goodness and truth; so turn the death that she gave me back on her. Take death from me now come on now. Don't tell me you're afraid of these evil bitches in the spiritual and physical realm?

Have I not suffered enough at the hands of the wicked and evil in the spiritual and physical realm?

No Lovey, look at my life and tell me; have I not suffered enough?

So why are you allowing this evil to continue to happen to me?

Why are you continuing to allow them to hurt me?

Why the hell should I bow down to her?

She's not you and could never be you. I will not bow down to her in the living nor in death. She can kiss my royal brown ass. She's the one to bow down to me and kiss my stinky feet. No better yet clean my shit. Dyam bright on har part. No Lovey, disya female death bright eeen. Dyam crasses fi real.

No, Lovey don't laugh. How dare her? Come on now

You Lovey have my record of truth as well as my good will. I WILL NOT CHANGE WHAT IS WRITTEN IN ANY OF THESE BOOKS TO PLEASE THE WICKED AND EVIL OF THIS WORLD. THEY AND MY

FAMILY CAN CONDEMN ME, BUT I WILL NOT CHANGE WHAT IS WRITTEN TO PLEASE THEM.

YOU SHOWED ME THEM LOVEY AND I TOLD OTHERS OF WHAT YOU'VE SHOWN ME.

NOTHING IN THESE BOOKS ARE FABRICATED; NOR ARE THEY TALES. YES I HAVE MY FUN AND PLAY IN SOME OF THEM; THESE BOOKS, BUT THEY ARE OUR TRUTH. SO WHY WOULD I CHANGE WHAT I'VE WRITTEN AND MAKE YOU AND ME AND OR I OUT TO BE A LIAR LOVEY?

You've told me what you want me to teach and I've done so. It was written on the school wall, "**FOR GOD SO LOVE US, HE IS WORTHY TO BE PRAISE.**"

I got so upset at you for the loving so despite you showing me how great loving us so is.

I also got upset and or down on you about this because as humans we are to know better. You should not have to remind us of your true love for us.

I told you, my true love is greater than yours because I don't love so; I love true and you see and know this.

You've seen my tears for you and I've cussed you out rude and proper. As humans we say we love you but yet we hurt you reckless and rude.

So why should you have to remind us of your love of truth? Come on now.

We are the ones to destroy you come on now. This is why no one can tell me about love or say they love me, because it's the ones that say they love you that cheat on you, set you up, rob you of your financial well being and health; some even kill you. So fuck love and all who say they love. **<u>Love is truly not greater than true love.</u>**

True love truly cares.

True love watches over you.

True love shares and true love definitely do not go out of their way to hurt you or others.

<u>*True love grows; thus truth is everlasting life.*</u>

Truth I say and true love all the way.

Lovey, humans have and has classed you low.

We've classed you so low that I've had to ask you, if this is the legacy you want for yourself? No one should have to disrespect you and class you lower than filth come on now.

SO NO, I WILL NOT DO THIS; TAKE BACK WHAT I'VE WRITTEN, NOR WILL I APOLOGIZE TO ANYONE.

You are my God and truth. You are not death; you are life; good and true life. It's us as humans that did not choose properly. We let the dirty scumbags of the church otherwise known as clergy tell us bullshit about you so that the devil and or death might find favour in them.

They rob humanity of you and your truth Lovey.

They rob you of your truth Lovey and distort it to sell their evil agenda, thus they tell humanity about profits; woops prophets come on now.

There gods are not you Lovey thus I call their gods shit. I want and need none of them because death and I are truly not friends and you know this Lovey come on now.

So fuck all of them; everyone that will be against me; those wretched demons that will now set me and my family up to disgrace me and kill them. And Lovey, if my entire family want to condemn me, call

me evil and all the evil words in the world, if they; my entire family want to disassociate themselves from me then so be it. I've told you Lovey, I can walk away from family and trust me I will not have any regret. Yes I will be hurt but you know what Lovey, I truly have you because I've learnt to rely on you for everything. You are my pain reliever at times so no; I care not if family condemn me. Just let them know; they had better know that their condemnation is for life because absolutely nothing they do can or will get me to return after the dust has and have cleared with me.

All wen dem a ded anna call mi, mi hear an def si an bline because trust me; I will see them and the hell they choose and chose for self and I will leave their ass there in hell without regret. Soh dem forewarned beforehand come on now. Many in this family know truth; the spiritual truth, but yet fail to rely on it. Too dyam stuck up an stush. I welcome my spiritual eye with you Lovey and trust me; I aim on keeping it

forever ever without end with you come on now.

You want an apology; my ass is there, fucking kiss it. That's your apology.

So no matter I see the demon duppy and scapegoats for the Illuminati (Jay Z, Kanye West and Barack Obama) I will not fair them. Like I said, when they are burning like a bitch in hell I will be with you Lovey. I do not care if they set me up with the Canadian Government and do all to me for me to come their way; I will not worship them or come their way. Fuck them because death is not life, death is death and they're fucking dead. I don't know how the hell someone can say they love their family; children, mother and father and sell them out to death.

Some of you sell out your friends because you think there is going to be a New World Order where death and or Satan rules. **SATAN SOLD YOUR ASSES TO DEATH AND CONDEMNED YOUR ASSES INCLUDING THE LIVES OF YOUR CHILDREN AND FAMILY MEMBERS TO HELL WITHOUT YOU KNOWING IT.**

THE LAW PLAINLY STATES, **"THE WAGES OF SIN IS DEATH."** So where are you going to go with your bullshit?

Just as Eve; Evening got locked out of Lovey's abode indefinitely, so are the lots of you locked out. You kill for financial gain; profit. **THUS NOAH'S ARK WILL BE UPON LAND REAL SOON.**

Some of you are literally going to die of medical need.

Lack of food and water

War and famine

Diseases

Nuclear radiation and so much more.

Some of you are going to be killed and eaten by other humans on a massive scale literally. So truly good luck from 2016 onwards because life on earth have and has reached critical mass.

Therefore, earth and the elements of earth must turn against humans; all who are wicked and evil. ***However and or but, she Mother Earth and the elements of earth must provide for the good people of the earth; the good and true seeds Lovey has and have given me.*** *Lovey must now separate good from evil and let Satan and or Death provide for their wicked and evil own come on now. Allelujah, Glory. This is truly your day My Beloved and*

King. You are my Lovey and you are more than worthy to be praised.

So for all of you rats that truly do not know; Satan cannot tell you that he's going to sacrifice a child of God because **_LOVEY WOULD NEVER SACRIFICE HIS CHILD FOR ANY OF YOU. YOU'RE ALL WICKED AND EVIL AND LOVEY HAS NOTHING TO DO WITH UNCLEAN PEOPLE._**

YOU ARE DEATH'S AND OR SATAN'S SACRIFICE AND WILL ALWAYS BE HIS SACRIFICE UNTO DEATH COME ON NOW.

No don't look at my turmoil. I had to go through this because I was set so. But my time has come to hand back death to death. And on this day, December 29th, 2015, I hand back death his death. I truly do not want or need his or her bullshit. I am not death; thus justice must prevail over all who are unjust and it matters not if you are a god or spirit that is wicked and evil. As long as you are unjust justice must prevail over you.

I deal in good and true life; thus I accept truth and live for truth. Yes I know the end of all who are wicked and evil, but for the good and pure at heart; there is truly no end come on now. Yes I talked to you Lovey about this; all that I dreamt, and it's like you're telling me not to worry about what the devil is doing. So I am not going to worry about wicked and evil people; I am going to let you handle them Lovey. Therefore, I put my health, financial well being, stresses, issues and concerns, my good up good up life with you and me in your strong, good and capable hands for more than protection and safety. You are my good security Lovey; so truly secure me and my family including the good up good up seeds of truth and goodness you've given me. I trust you to strike down all who hurts me by turning back their evils back on them.

I am doing your work Lovey and I have to live as Psalms One. I cannot commune with the living and walking dead; wicked and evil anymore. So as death handed me death, <u>I hand them back their death; that which death has and have given me on this your day Lovey; December 29, 2015.</u> Every nation and follower of death must return to death. Death must claim them because in truth, death has nothing to do with me nor does death have anything to do with you.

I cannot live for death and in truth; I truly do not want or need anything from death. So I don't know why death is giving me death and I truly don't want it.

There is no Jesus here.
There is no hurt and pain here.
There are no lies here.
No stress here.

If humans truly cared about self and others; they would not kill each other or hate each other. This planet is big enough for all Lovey, but time and time again we as humans have and has proven to you that we cannot live in peace and true peace with each other.

Instead of preserving life we take life; all life.

Instead of saying we want to live; we go against life and take all from life. So I truly cannot worry about wicked and evil people. When I see all of this Lovey, I have to come to you and I've come to you. Thus I said to you, absolutely no forgiveness on my day for wicked and evil people. You can forgive them on your day Lovey, which is December 29th, but absolutely no forgiveness on my day.

<u>Further, you see what this dutty stinking jezebel try du to mi on your day, an yu would forgive these nasty people. Lovey, wen mi bow down to har, mi nuh lose yu?</u>

When mi bow down to har; mi naah tell yu sey yu a count out and mi nuh count yu?

When mi bow down to har, mi naah tell yu sey mi nuh want or need yu?

When mi bown down to har, am I not telling you that all you and my mother has and have done for me; I did not appreciate it?

Am I not breaking my good up good up true vow to you wen mi bow down to har?

Would I not be like the rest of them; ancestors of then and now including all of humanity?

Suh wey dis BC demon duppy a try Lovey?

Yu noa wha I yu mi fi cuss.

No, I should cuss you fi let dis dutty dog wey a more than showboat fi man and or the demons of hell fi cum bright up harself with mi.

Lovey, a soh yu tan?

A soh yu really tan?

Coo pan mi and yu let har eene fi cum trouble mi an cut mi?

Lovey, yu mek har cut mi soh?

A soh yu hate mi fi har fi cum cut me soh?

No a war yu want with mi Lovey.

Lovey you truly want us to go to war?

No, you truly don't want to war with me because I've told you time and time again, I am the one with the brutal temper and your temper is truly not fierce as mine. I am your daughter and not because I am quiet like you should you trouble me. The saying goes, "when the lion is sleeping do not try and wake him." I guess this sketel did not learn this.

No, this cussing shi get anno cussing; thus she had truly better thank you Lovey. Yes this is your day and I went brutal but this is me when provoked. I make no apologies thus Lovey thank you for me.

No, this is truly not real Lovey.

But fi real Lovey, yu mek this damn ugly wuss dan cesspool of all di shit wey pile up inna earth cum cut mi?

Coo pan har tu; an yu mek har cut mi!!! Then yu have the nerve and audacity fi let di Illuminati trolls of hell fine mi.

Bo wait Lovey, evil a mock yu an mi?

Lovey, you are my good choice and you're letting evil taunt me like this?

Evil a tell mi sey yu wutless and powerless because they can reach me at will and there isn't a damned thing you Lovey can do about it.

Lovey, is this truly for real?

No, I truly need not say more because this is surreal to claate.

You're not real when it comes to evil finding me and tormenting me.

Was this what I've been preparing myself for all this time?

Is this what's become of us Lovey for evil to reach me and taunt me about you?

<u>Why is evil tormenting me by showing me that you are weak and powerless when it comes to them?</u>

Did I not tell you; I do not want or need a weak God and you're not listening to me when I talk?

Lovey, can the true and devoted hurt each other like this?

Can true and devoted lie to each other Lovey?

No right?

So why are you allowing evil to hurt me?

I truly don't know anymore with you Lovey?

HOW CAN YOU AS LOVEY AND MY BELOVED DISAPPOINT ME LIKE THIS?

I ASKED YOU FOR GOODNESS AND I UPLOADED MY GOOD AND TRUE WILL AND I NEED ON LULU.COM AND ALL I GOT RETURNED TO ME IS PURE EVIL.

Lovey, why should good be repaid in evil?

Lovey, why should anyone do good if they are going to get evil in return?

This is wrong Lovey. Good should be returned to good when they do good come on now.

Why return evil for good?

ARE YOU NOT TELLING THE PERSON TO STOP DOING GOOD?

Are you not saying you favour evil over good?
Ah Lovey, I know what you are telling me and or trying to say to me and I over stand.

Lovey no one should feel abandoned by you. So the practice of doing good and receiving evil in return should stop. It has to stop Lovey.

THERE SHOULD BE NO EVIL COST ATTACHED TO GOODNESS COME ON NOW.

People are trying Lovey, so why should they receive evil for their efforts?

Why the hell should evil find a way in and disrupt our happy home?

Evil should not stop and or hinder good and true people Lovey come on now.

Make this a new law on your day that no evil should hinder the good that are trying to get to you. No evil should put stumbling blocks in our way come on now.

Why should we cry due to the evil of others Lovey?

Come on now tell me. You are my true hope and devoted and you're going to let evil come in and steal me away from you. This is truly not a test, this is willfully done Lovey.

This is a deliberate and willful act on the part of evil and you are going to allow this?

GOOD AND EVIL

You cannot let this go unpunished Lovey.

Did I ever tell you I want to be on the side of evil?

No, don't answer that because I've told you I feel as if I am on the wrong side and I want to leave you.

Now you see why sometimes I tell you I want to leave you. You keep allowing evil into my life come on now.

Lovey, yu really mek shi du dis?

Lovey, yu mek dis crabbit cum du dis?

Wait, what are you telling me Lovey?

Are you telling me you don't want me anymore and you're going to let female evil come in on me and do her damage?

Lovey yu wicked tu mi to yass.

No, fi real fi yu fi du dis.

Yu really wicked to mi.

Lovey, yu really du dis without baxing dung di demon duppy?

No Lovey, I am crying condemnation now. Lock up female death tu and burn di key.

Shi caane cumma hinda mi. Lock har up because what she did, she willingly did it. Shi cut mi pan purpose because I did not want to bow down to her. ***So as Male Death is locked away in the fires of hell so must Female Death be locked away in the fires of hell.*** So Lovey on this day, your day; condemn Female Death for what she did and give her the same punishment as Satan, Sin and Death including the demons and people of hell combined. Close all doors to them now man come on now. I'm hurting Lovey and not them or you.

Let it truly be over for all facets of death and their people on your day, December 29th, 2015 come on now.

You struggled so hard and long with me to have evil continuously putting doubt in my head when it comes to you. Shut them down now Lovey come on now.

You are my truth and true love; so why should I let anyone come in and steal you from me. I am not my ancestors. ***Goodness begets goodness no matter how hard our struggles come on now.***

I struggled long and hard and you're the one I go to with all. So yes, put an end to Female Death just as you've put an end to Male Death; Satan and his hosts and children; family. Yes I know this is truly not the way you wanted things to go, but it has to go this way.

Good and Evil should live in peace but we truly cannot Lovey. One cannot be building good and the other destroying it all. It will not work and it isn't working. <u>Evil want and need their own domain where they can control it all; so give it to them. But ensure evil cannot spread beyond that which you've given them. Therefore, we need to have impenetrable frameworks and foundations set up where evil is truly contained and cannot get out ever again.</u> We have to contain evil Lovey lest we have nothing. Come on now.

Further, you cannot fight for people and children that truly do not want you Lovey. I talk about my abuse, but what about your abuse Lovey? **<u>Truly listen to All Things Are Working because you too get the short end of the stick when it comes to humanity.</u>**

Humanity couldn't care less about you; thus humanity seek ways to disprove you. But it's so weird Lovey, in all that humans are doing to disprove and disgrace you; they are looking for a saving grace from you. Go figure. Now tell me Lovey, how does this work?

<u>Humans don't want you but yet they want you to save them from their sins; wicked and evil ways. If you don't want Lovey, why should Lovey save you?</u>

Your choice was not Lovey; so Lovey truly cannot save you come on now.

<u>We as humans hurt you Lovey; so truly think of your good and true well being. It's not all about humans alone Lovey, it's about good and true life everywhere including you.</u>

So yes, I know your hurt and pain and it's sad that we as humans cannot see the pain we've caused you.

Creation is beautiful, but when creation becomes tainted then it becomes truly ugly.

The mess that humans created is ugly.

Lives were lost Lovey and lives are still being lost; so I don't know why you would want to hold on to people that truly don't care about you.

YOU HAVE TO DO WHAT'S BEST FOR ALL BUT YOU CAN NO LONGER DO WHAT'S BEST FOR WICKED AND EVIL PEOPLE.

You gave us a choice thus will and we are the ones to follow evil and do all that is wicked and evil. None chose to do good and religion don't make you good; it just makes you unclean; dirty and on holy.

No one can be just and righteous in an unclean system Lovey. You and I both know this; therefore, I stay in my little corner and do that which I can do to help you truthfully. Come on now.

Yes I know this is not the end, but I am encouraging you to think of you and good life including me. It's wrong for humans to destroy good life; thus truly close off all the portals of evil and death to me, my family and our good and true people; seeds more than infinitely and indefinitely forever ever without end for more than infinite and indefinite lifetimes and generations to come. Evil must no longer reach me Lovey, nor should it reach my children and my family; whether living or dead including the good up good up seeds you've given me whether living or dead. Let goodness and truth reach me at all times; thus, let the closure to me from all facets of evil and wickedness be like that of the spiritual realm where evil cannot get over to the side of our good and true people. My gates and surrounding must be impenetrable to evil people and spirits including the wicked and evil elements that surrounds evil.

Oh yeah Lovey you owe me big time.

No it's not wha. You owe me and I want and need to be compensated big time for what you have done.

Yes I went there and you are going to pay. I am upset, no not upset but disappointed in you for allowing this happen; evil wreaking havoc in my life from December 26 to today; December 29th, 2015.

Lovey evil has nothing to do with us; so truly let evil leave me alone. All this havoc does take a toll on me in the physical world; realm.

Lovey in truth, if evil wanted good for self; evil wouldn't hate, war and kill; destroy all in their path. Life is truly worth it despite the obstacles in our way.

Humans have and has proven to you time and time again that they cannot live in peace; nor can we be trusted to live peacefully with each other. Lies do come into play and many nations lie on each other just to create strife. Thus I say unto you, if you find me unjust in all that I've written forgive me and void all that which you find unjust.

You know better than me Lovey and I am not the final sayer in all of this you are; thus you have your day.

And as always, never forget my truth of you and my beautiful and gorgeous mother. You're both my true stay and true life. I will always truly love the both of you true. So never forget truth in all that you do.

And as I close this book, I close it in the goodness and truth of you and my mother, my children and family and the good up good up seeds you've given me. Lovey no matter what evil do to me, you will always be within me and with me; my choice and tomorrow. You are my safe and safe keep always never forget this.

So stay encouraged and think of you from time to time because it will always be you. So as we journey on in truth, let's vacation in 2016 together. All that is wicked and evil including wicked and evil systems truly let them begin to crumble and pass away.

Earth need to be renewed and we must renew her void of all wicked and evil.

She too deserve to be at peace and rest with you and her surroundings Lovey. So as you help me in goodness and in truth, help her in goodness and truth as well as the universe; help the universe in goodness and in truth to drive out all that is wicked and evil in him.

Michelle

OTHER BOOKS BY MICHELLE JEAN

Blackman Redemption – The Fall of Michelle Jean
Blackman Redemption – After the Fall Apology
Blackman Redemption – World Cry – Christine Lewis
Blackman Redemption
Blackman Redemption – The Rise and Fall of Jamaica
Blackman Redemption – The War of Israel
Blackman Redemption – The Way I Speak to God
Blackman Redemption – A Little Talk With Man
Blackman Redemption – The Den of Thieves
Blackman Redemption – The Death of Jamaica
Blackman Redemption – Happy Mother's Day
Blackman Redemption – The Death of Faith
Blackman Redemption – The War of Religion
Blackman Redemption – The Death of Russia
Blackman Redemption – The Truth
Blackman Redemption – Spiritual War
Blackman Redemption – The Youths
Blackman Redemption – Black Man Where Is Your God?

The New Book of Life
The New Book of Life – A Cry For The Children
The New Book of Life – Judgement
The New Book of Life – Love Bound
The New Book of Life – Me
The New Book of Life – Life

Just One of Those Days
Book Two – Just One of Those Days
Just One of Those Days – Book Three The Way I Feel
Just One of Those Days – Book Four

The Days I Am Weak
Crazy Thoughts – My Book of Sin
Broken
Ode to Mr. Dean Fraser

A Little Little Talk
A Little Little Talk – Book Two

Prayers
My Collective
A Little Talk/A Time For Fun and Play
Simple Poems
Behind The Scars
Songs of Praise And Love

Love Bound
Love Bound – Book Two

Dedication Unto My Kids
More Talk
Saving America From A Woman's Perspective
My Collective the Other Side of Me
My Collective the Dark Side of Me
A Blessed Day
Lose To Win
My Doubtful Days – Book One

My Little Talk With God
My Little Talk With God – Book Two

A Different Mood and World – Thinking

My Nagging Day

GOOD AND EVIL

My Nagging Day – Book Two
Friday September 13, 2013
My True Love
It Would Be You
My Day

A Little Advice – Talk
1313, 2032, 2132 – The End of Man
Tata

MICHELLE'S BOOK BLOG – BOOKS 1 – 22

My Problem Day
A Better Way
Stay – Adultery and the Weight of Sin – Cleanliness
Message

Let's Talk
Lonely Days – Foundation
A Little Talk With Jamaica – As Long As I Live
Instructions For Death
My Lonely Thoughts
My Lonely Thoughts – Book Two
My Morning Talks – Prayers With God
What A Mess
My Little Book
A Little Word With You
My First Trip of 2015
Black Mother – Mama Africa
Islamic Thought
My California Trip January 2015
My True Devotion by Michelle – Michelle Jean
My Many Questions To God

My Talk
My Talk Book Two
My Talk Book Three – The Rise of Michelle Jean
My Talk Book Four
My Talk Book Five
My Talk Book Six
My Talk Book Seven
My Talk Book Eight – My Depression
My Talk Book Nine – Death
My Talk Book Ten – Wow
My Day – Book Two
My Talk Book Eleven – What About December?
Haven Hill
What About December – Book Two
My Talk Book Twelve – Summary and or Confusion
My Talk Book Thirteen
My Talk Book Fourteen – My Talk With God
My Talk Book Fifteen – My Talk
My Thoughts – Freedom
My Heart to Heart With Lovey – God

Letters to my song and words of praise and truth; My true and unconditional Love; Lovey, Good God and Allelujah

Caged
Why
I Don't Know But I Know
Our Journey/My Anger
Real Situation
December 2015
Confusion or Confession
My Good and True Will and I Need